50 Things You Should Know Before Marrying a Filipina Girlfriend

TOPICS

Contents

HIS STORY	6
HER STORY	10
THE COUNTRY	13
1. Island Living	13
2. Hot or Not	15
3. Filipino English	18
4. Country of Extremes	19
5. Religion	22
6. Transportation	23
7. Organized Chaos	25
8. Currency	27

THE CULTURE 28

9. Pasalubong — 28

10. Game On — 29

11. Holidays and Fiestas — 32

12. Christmas — 34

13. Hospitality — 36

15. Pouty Point — 39

16. Language Nuances — 42

17. Balikbayan Box — 45

18. Smile! You're on Camera — 47

19. Eyebrows Up — 49

20. Teasing — 50

21. Talk of the Town — 52

22. Will you Marry Me? — 54

23. Small Talk / Pleasantries — 55

24. Hello, Eat — 56

25. Romantics at Heart — 58

26. Bro-mance — 60

27. Karaoke	62
28. Laugh Out Loud	63
29. Rich and Famous	64
30. Price of Fame	65
31. Whitening Stuff	68
32. Birthday Treat	72
33. Conservative	75
34. PDA	76
35. Bless	77
36. Loud Voice	79
37. Confrontation	80
38. Filipino Time	81
39. Filipino Food	83
40. Gratitude to Parents	85
41. Bayanihan	86
42. Pamamanhikan	87

THE GIRL 89

43. Soap Opera	89

44. He said, She Said	91
45. Single Living with Parents	92
46. Yaya	93
SOME THINGS TO CONSIDER	**95**
47. Real Filipina	95
48. Street Food	97
49. Bottled Water	99
50. Plug-In Ready	100
ABOUT THE AUTHORS	**101**
LOVE STORY IN A NUTSHELL	**101**

A Guide for Non-Filipinos

The topics in this book apply to Filipinos in general terms. It is not meant to stereotype Filipinos, and should not be construed in any way as truth for all Filipinos. Everyone is unique, and certainly your Filipina (Pinay) girlfriend's response to a situation would vary depending on where she was raised (city or province/country side) and how she was raised.

Hopefully, this book will ease the culture shock you might have in visiting a country that is different from your own, and help you understand your girlfriend's background, and why she acts, talks, and responds the way she does.

Some topics include short anecdotes from the authors' personal experiences.

His Story

There I was in a room by myself, never thinking I would be one of them, sitting there reflecting back on all the dates I have been on that ended in disaster.

Just when I thought a date might workout, she goes and pinches me throughout an entire movie leaving multiple bruises on my arms. I had to hold her hand, not out of romantic passion but out of sheer fear that it is possible I may not make it out of the theater alive. Maybe it was her way of saying that a movie on the first date is a bad idea. With her disappointment and my agonizing pain, needless to say that first date was the last.

Then there was that time I went on a blind date where I drove 50 miles not knowing what the girl looked like. Great personality, but short on looks… very short… I believe you should at least have some attraction for the person you date, and it just wasn't there! Note to self, no more blind dates!

The list goes on and on from being cheated to plain and simple "not clicking." So there I was… my twenties almost over and my thirties closing in, and a love life nowhere to be found. After years of disappointments, discouragement starts to set in, and I think to myself in that room, could it be true? Am I about to resort to such tactics!? Am I about to punch the keys of desperation!? Am I about to leap into unknown territory where I never thought I would go!? YES! I went ahead with my covert operation and earned the certificate of an online dater! <sigh>

As I accepted the fact and kept it top secret, I proceeded in my tedious task of looking for Mrs. Right! I filled out my profile as well as what I was looking for in a potential "dream girl," clicked the button and presto!! The search was on... Nope, no way! Whoa, she uses a lot of foul language! No way, what? What is she wearing?? God, no!

Day 1 is over. Day 2, 3, and 4 go pretty much the same, until the 5th day. I'm scrolling the profiles and pics thinking to myself... maybe I am meant to be single like... I don't know... forever? Then a picture appeared like something out of a fairytale, and I verbalize out loud to myself in that lonely, small, dark, depressing room, "WOW!" My eyes widened, my heart began to race. I continued to stare at her brown skin, brown eyes, jet black hair, and gorgeous Asian features. I scrolled down to read her profile... yes... yup, that's good, that is great! It's a match! Could it be? Could it truly be? Is it possible that she could be... the ONE?!

As wedding bells were ringing in my ears, I scrolled

down to see where she is located. I know here in Georgia there is no one for me! I began to read, not the state from where she might reside, but the country!! Philippines... 6000 miles away!

After I picked myself up off the floor, I had a decision to make. Am I going to continue on my discouraging search or am I going to pursue? Obviously, I pursued and it turned out to be worthwhile! After nervously emailing, which led to phone calls, then to skyping for a whole year, never even seeing her physically, the day finally came and I was able to fly to the Philippines to meet her in person. After connecting already for a year, it was truly my... our dream come true!

At the time of this writing, we have been married for 5 awesome years, and have a three year old son, with a daughter that we're working on.

I've come to realize in the pursuit of my dream girl, I was not going to let distance or anything get in my way of what I knew in my heart was right. Little did I know that not only was it distance that I tried to cross, but there were other hurdles that needed to be jumped in order to make it successfully to the finish line. I realized in order to have a successful relationship with a Filipina (Pinay), you have to understand her culture.

Maybe you're in the same situation I was in, and you're thinking about dating a Pinay or building a relationship, or you just want to understand the culture better. Not only do you want to admire the beauty outwards, but you want to go in depth to be more prepared as to what to expect. This book will help you in your journey of building a meaningful relationship. Trust me, I wish I had known these pointers before I went to the Philippines. This isn't all there is, but this will help you understand your potential partner better, and show that you really care to learn them in every way.

Her Story

I was in my early thirties (yep, you read that right! My husband is four years younger than me!), and most of my friends around my age were already married with kids. My friends, my parents' friends, people who knew me who were concerned, and those who just wanted to meddle were "teasing" me and pairing me off to every available bachelor, or so it seemed. I was introduced to mostly good and God-fearing men. In the end, none of the "probable" relationships came to be, the Pinoys simply backed off. I was starting to think that there might be something wrong with me, until close friends told me that the Pinoys were simply intimidated. Filipino guys saw me as "high maintenance" simply because I had a successful career, I drove my own car, and I had a personal yaya (helper/maid).

I worked for an international research and development company that had expats working in the Philippines for months or years at a time. I was the company's "unofficial" tour guide. I toured the visiting expats, including the managing president and his wife to see the beautiful sights in my hometown. Most of my coworkers shied away from talking to our expats, simply because they were our "bosses." Even if the expat was from a different department than mine, some engineers asked me to help with the tour, and some expat friends referred other visiting expats to me for their city tour.

I never entertained the idea of dating a non-Filipino up until I dated one. It was very different from a relationship with a co-Pinoy. Less drama, more romance, and no giving me the cold shoulder and leaving me clueless as to why things weren't going right. Non-Filipinos would let you know straight up if something bothered them, or if there's something they want or do not want. It gets rid of the guessing part of the relationship.

It was also through that relationship that I learned to love my brown skin. That relationship however was short-lived, and my Mom (my parents already migrated to the US ahead of me) kept bugging me to create an account on an online dating site. And I'm like, really mom? Only desperate people do that! I'm having the time of life! I'm not desperate!

For two years she kept nagging me to go on a popular dating site. Out of nowhere I received an email from a Christian dating site. I didn't even know Christian dating sites existed! To satisfy my mom, and to be able to tell her to stop bugging me about it, I created an account. It was their tag line that reeled me in, "Let His heart lead yours." I prayed a short prayer, "Lord, if this is Your will, let the guy find me, and not me looking for him." Within a week, I got an email from this really good looking, and super-buffed guy who looked like he could punch a hole through a concrete wall. He is now my husband, and the rest is history.

The Country

1. Island Living
The Philippines has more than 7,000 islands. It is common knowledge that at least one of the islands go under water when high tide rolls in.

There are 3 major islands: Luzon, Visayas, and Mindanao. Customs and culture may vary depending on the area you visit.

There are 8 major dialects, and a lot of other ones in between. If you want to learn how to speak Filipino, then study Tagalog, which is understood throughout the country and also taught in schools. However, Tagalog is spoken mostly in Luzon. Cebuano (or Visayan) is the more dominant dialect spoken in Visayas and Mindanao. It is best to ask what dialect is spoken in the area you are visiting, and learn that.

Pronunciation
Luzon /*loo-zohn*/; Visayas /*vee-sah-yus*/; Mindanao /*min-dah-now*/; Cebuano /*seh-bwah-noh*/

Her Story
"High tide or low tide?" This is a popular response by Pinoys when asked how many islands are in the Philippines. It was popularized by a Ms. Philippines

contestant vying for Ms. Universe.

At least a couple of islands go under water when high tide comes in. There are also a number of shifting sand bars that "shift" in shape depending on the water currents.

Shifting sand bar – Photo credit: Christian "Eyean" Toledo

Manjuyod White Sandbar, Negros Island, Philippines
Photo credit: Kenny Russ Teves

2. Hot or Not

The Philippines has two seasons: wet and dry, based on the amount of rainfall. Wet or rainy season usually starts in November 'till February. It is best to visit during this time if you are sensitive to heat, since most homes in the Philippines do not have air conditioning. During rainy season, typical weather is sunny/cloudy during the day with rains in the afternoon.

Dry season is from March to October. April and May are considered the "summer" months, and kids are on summer school break. May is the hottest month of the year with temperatures averaging 93°F/34°C during the day and 77°F/25°C at night. January is the coolest month with high temperatures of 70°F/20°C, and low temperatures of 50°F/20°C. Also, since the Philippines is located close to the equator, sunrise is around 6 AM, and sunset at around 6PM. This stays pretty much the same day in and day out, with minor variations.

His Story

As I stated in the introduction, not only was I nervous and a bit overwhelmed about meeting my "dream girl" for the first time in person after skyping for a year, but I also started to have cold feet. Not the kind to where you are unsure if what you are about to do is right, but the kind to where you grab your socks because your feet are cold.

It was January 16 when I flew out to the Philippines. The temperature in Atlanta, Georgia, USA was in the mid-thirties the day of my flight, and roughly 19 hours later I found myself in a beautiful tropical climate around 70 °F. Huge difference in climate!

Having culture shock, meeting the girl of my dreams, as well as her parents (they flew to the Philippines to meet me - they live in California) was making me sweat. I did not need the thick clothing. Once I got settled and over the jet lag, it was wonderful. We even went snorkeling and went to the beach a time or two, in January!! Imagine that!

Traveler tip: Wear lighter clothes underneath so you can take off layers before arriving in the Philippines to avoid the appearance of being a "first timer," and most importantly, avoid heat stroke.

Her Story

Although the Philippines enjoys a hot and humid weather almost all year round, most homes do not have air conditioning or *aircon* as it is known locally. This is because it is costly to buy one, and the electric bill goes up fast. But for the more affluent families who can afford to have *aircon*, it is almost always a one-room AC unit, and not centralized air.

The same can be said of hot water not being centralized.

Most homes only have the regular tap water, which is cold if you're not used to it. And yes, most Pinoys take a cold shower; although some homes do have a hot water unit in the bathrooms.

3. Filipino English

The Philippines is the third largest English-speaking country in the world. English is used in government, commercial, and educational documents. English is also the medium of instruction in schools. This is one of the reasons for the call center boom in the Philippines.

For the most part, Filipinos understand English. However, most may not speak it fluently, or may not follow grammar rules, or may have an accent.

However, if somebody has difficulty expressing themselves in English and you have difficulty understanding what they are saying, it does not mean they are ignorant. It simply means that maybe they didn't attend a school that had good English teachers or they haven't been around English-speaking foreigners much, which make them less conversant in English.

4. Country of Extremes
The Philippines is a beautiful country where beautiful nature abounds. However, it is also a third world country of extremes. Picture a majestic entrance to a world class resort, and then just a few meters away is a small shack where a family lives.

If you visit cities like Manila or Cebu, you'll see high-rise buildings with offices for international companies, as well as expansive world-class malls where Filipinos like to congregate to escape the heat. But then you'll also see street kids running in between stopped vehicles, and knocking on the windows begging for money.

His Story
I was sitting in the passenger seat of my (then) fiancée's car, waiting for the light to turn green, just enjoying each other's company when our fun, loving, romantic conversation got interrupted by a knock on my window. As I turned to see what in the world could be interrupting my romantic moment, I was surprised to see a half dressed boy around 10 years old with dirty face and hands staring at me, looking sad. Right there and then I had mixed feelings about it... part of me felt sorry for the boy, then there was the other part that wanted to freak out because a dirty-faced, beady eyed boy stared into my eyes like he wasn't going away until I gave him something.

All I could think about was the old movie "Children of the Corn." We'll just say the ending to that movie wasn't pleasant.

So all of this took place at a stop light for about 60 secs, which felt like an eternity. Chad said whatever you do, don't look at him. I'm thinking... uhh... too late! She said to knock on the window and he will go away. Once I took her suggestion and knocked, it was so easy. The boy left just like that.

Usually, the boy is sent by others, possibly family or friends that have him beg for money. Most of the time it is a staged act so they can go waste money gambling, etc. which is why she said to knock back. It's way too common here. Light turned green. Thank God, only ten more lights to go. Oh no!

Her Story
The Philippine government doesn't condone giving to street kids and beggars because once you give, it only encourages them to keep begging and it becomes a pitiful cycle. Most cities have an anti-mendicancy law in place, which simply means that one can be prosecuted for giving to beggars.

Ironic, right? It is better to give donations to charitable institutions, orphanages, or churches that can put the money to better use for the needy. If you can't resist the beady-eyed look, you can give food instead of money.

Welcoming smile of a Filipino kid. – Photo credit: Kenny Russ Teves

5. Religion

The Philippines is predominantly Catholic, which is comprised by 80% of the country's population. If you were to ask someone what their religion is, they'd either say I'm Catholic, or I'm a Christian, or I'm Muslim.

Although Catholics are also Christians, commonly, if somebody says they are "Christian," it implies they are Baptist, Lutherans, non-denominational or "born-again" Christians, and other sects that believe in Jesus Christ. Some may also be Protestants.

11% of the population are Muslims and practice Islam. One can also be a Buddhist and a Catholic at the same time, although this is rare, but typical in the Filipino-Chinese community.

6. Transportation

Having a vehicle is considered more of a luxury than a necessity, and taking public transportation is common. Consider yourself lucky if your girlfriend or her family owns a vehicle. Otherwise, you can take the jeepney/jeep, bus, tricycle, or taxi depending on the public transport available in the city or town you are visiting. Some cities still have *tartanilla* or a carriage drawn by horses, but this is getting rare.

Also, most women in the Philippines do not drive. Statistics say male drivers outnumber female drivers five to one.

Pronunciation
tartanilla */tar-tah-nil-yuh/*

His Story
For the most part, everyone knows what a taxi, bus, jeep, or even a tricycle is… but what in the world is a jeepney? To me, the seating of a jeepney reminds me of a military style or SWAT vehicle to where the people sit inside along the walls of the vehicle facing each other. It can be awkward at times; especially if you are the only white boy in there. The outside however, can be colorful and decorative. It has the look of a small, really small bus with a back door that remains open all the time.

Sometimes, if there is no more available seating, you can see some folks just hang on from the back of the jeepney.

Her Story

The original jeepneys were remnants of the 2nd world war from US military jeeps that were left behind. Jeepneys or jeeps nowadays are longer, with some that can seat up to 30 people in the back. Riding the jeep is one of the cheapest modes of transportation in the Philippines, and can be an adventure in itself.

Colorful jeepney – Photo credit: Meynard Simborio

7. Organized Chaos

Traffic in the Philippines is organized chaos. You'll hear cars honking everywhere. Most Jeepney drivers would honk to attract passengers. Drivers are not being rude; they are simply honking other drivers or passengers to signal "Hey, I'm here!"

The average speed in the Philippines is s-l-o-w with most driving at 40 kmph/25 mph within the city and 60-100 kmph/35-60 mph on the highways. Speed limit signs are not a common sight. Pinoys tend to drive slower when there's more vehicles on the road, and faster when there's less. You simply go with the flow.

His Story
Here in the US, if someone honks it's because they are mad at you for cutting them off, etc. My first ride in Chad's car was scary, yet exciting! However, my very first thought when she picked me up from the airport and we started our drive was, are there any traffic laws here? I noticed there were lanes but not many cars were staying in them.

To my amazement, people were driving right down the middle of the lines, not in the lanes! On top of that, everyone was honking repeatedly at each other. I was thinking, I know I'm not the best driver around, but people here are hard core rebels; not only breaking traffic laws, but honking consistently at each other. Then what really tops the cake is Chad starts honking, as well as driving in the middle of the road (on the white line). Wow! She's one of them! Will I even survive three weeks here in the Philippines? I began to wonder...

8. Currency

The Philippine currency is called Peso, and the paper money is color-coded for easy recognition. You can have your currency exchanged at banks or you can also find currency exchange booths inside most shopping malls.

Most business places do not accept the US dollar or other foreign currency, and not all places accept credit cards, especially if you visit the province (country side). Be sure to have cash in pesos at all times.

Color-coded Philippine currency: Peso – Photo credit: Meynard Simborio

The Culture

9. Pasalubong
This is very typical of Pinoys when they travel; they always bring back souvenir items or food as gifts when they return. It's also very common to hear folks asking for *pasalubong* if they knew you just got back from a trip.

Your girlfriend's family might expect you to bring *pasalubong* when you visit. Although items like perfume, purses, clothes, shoes, and so on are preferred (especially for your gf), but chocolates for everyone are a sure winner too.

Pronunciation
pasalubong */puh-suh-loo-bong/*

Her Story
I did not ask my husband (then fiance') to bring me any gift nor did I tell him about our culture of *pasalubong*. But it was really sweet of him to give me a white gold bracelet with pink sapphire and diamonds on it (pink is my favorite color) as an engagement gift when he came down to the Philippines. My parents didn't care about *pasalubong* either. They were just so happy and excited to marry me off!

10. Game On

Filipinos are fans of basketball, and more recently boxing. Filipino men love to play basketball, usually in their own home made single ring courts.

Boxing is a more recent favorite. Families and friends would get together to watch the greatest boxing champ in the world, Manny Pacquiao. Watching Manny is such a big hit that even some government officials rent out gymnasiums and setup huge TVs so that the entire neighborhood can watch the boxing bout.

Other common recreation are watching movies, going to the beach, and window-shopping at the mall.

His Story
When I first heard of Manny Pacquiao it was shortly after my wife and I got married. She told me about his humble beginnings and how he fought his way up in rank to become a world-class boxing champ. Little did I know how much Pinoys really support him, and rally together to watch his fights. It is a known fact that crime drops to almost 0 in the Philippines during a Pacquiao fight. Even criminals and troublemakers drop their schemes to watch Manny fight. My hats off to Manny for not only winning the fight in the ring, but outside the ring as well without him throwing a punch! Maybe if he had fights every day, the Philippines will be crime free!

I have seen two of Manny's fights on TV. We were in California visiting my wife's parents and we all got invited over to someone's house to watch the fight. Every time Manny threw a punch, the cheers were loud! Our son just turned two at that time, and he cried every time they cheered.

It was funny in a way because all the 20 or so people there would feel bad and apologize for screaming so loud, just to do it again within a couple of minutes. Needless to say, my son was traumatized by his first Pinoy Pacquiao fight experience. I was told by a couple of them that the last time they got together to watch a Pacquiao fight, they got the cops called on them for being too loud. So when I say that they know how to get together and fellowship, they really do! And that's not a bad thing... well, I guess until the cops come!

My second time to watch Manny's fight was here in Georgia where my wife and I live. My wife found out there was a get together at someone's house not far from where we live. Although she only knew a few people there, it was an open door for her to "invite herself and me" over after asking a friend who knew the hosts. And they were such good hosts and very welcoming!

We asked my parents to watch our son because we knew

what was coming this time. The house we went to was in a cul-de-sac and I was amazed that the entire circle, even in the middle going down the entire street was packed with cars! Once we made our way through the car maze into the house there were literally a hundred or so people in what looked like a 2500 sq. ft. house. People were watching on multiple TVs within the house and even outside in the backyard. I remember thinking... this totally reminds me of the Philippines. There was one black guy, three white guys including myself (all husbands of Pinays), and then 90 to 95 Pinoys.

Food was overflowing too! All those yummy Filipino food and desserts filled the table and just kept filling up as people came in and brought food enough to feed an army!

11. Holidays and Fiestas

Filipinos are very religious. The country has a number of non-working holidays that honor a religious person or event.

November 1, which is All Soul's Day is observed as a national holiday for the dead, where people flock to graveyards to "visit" relatives who have passed away. The week of Easter is observed as the Holy Week. If you are visiting a province or country side during this time, you might catch a glimpse of a re-enactment of Jesus walking down the streets, carrying a cross, being flogged, on the way to be crucified.

Catholics celebrate fiestas all year round in honor of a patron saint. Fiestas are very festive and usually involve a street parade that has a *mar di gras* feel, except that the dances performed in the streets are in honor of Mary (mother of Jesus); the Sto. Niño, which represents the baby Jesus; a saint; and so on. The day of the fiesta varies on which part of the country you visit.

Another common theme that you will see if you take public transportation is a picture or a statue of Mary or the Sto. Niño.

Pinoys generally attribute their achievements and successes to God. "God bless" and "Thank God" is commonly said. "God bless" is usually used when ending a personal e-mail, chat, or other form of correspondence.

Sinulog: An annual cultural and religious festival in honor of the Sto. Niño, held every third Sunday of January in Cebu City, Philippines
Photo credit: Kenny Russ Teves

Pronunciation
Sinulog /see-noo-law-g/

12. Christmas

Christmas season is celebrated the longest in the Philippines. Filipinos hang Christmas decorations during the "ber" months (September to December) and way into the third week of January when the Three Kings were believed to visit the baby Jesus. You may hear Christmas music playing as early as September.

Although much of the Christmas decorations now are taken from Western culture, there are still elements that are uniquely Pinoy. One such element is the *Parol*, which is a lantern shaped like a star. There are many variations of the *parol*, with the more expensive ones made out of *capiz* (mother of pearl) shells. The sizes also vary from handheld ones to the gigantic. The *Parol* is very colorful, with the more modern ones installed with LED that lights up in synch to the music.

Another common sight during Christmas is the *Belen*, a depiction of the Nativity with Joseph, Mary, the baby Jesus in a manger, three wise men, shepherds, sheep, and the Star of Bethlehem.

Filipino-Chinese communities celebrate New Year twice: on December 31 and during the Chinese New Year in February.

Pronunciation

parol /*pah-rohl*/; capiz /*kah-peas*/; Belen /*beh-lehn*/

Parol: A star-shaped Christmas lantern – Photo credit: Christian "Eyean" Toledo

13. Hospitality

Filipinos are known to be hospitable and always offer the best to visitors. When having company over, some even offer their room or bed to a visitor, and sleep elsewhere in the house or on the floor.

When you eat out at a fast food chain like Jollibee or McDonald's, you don't have to clean up after yourself. There is staff assigned to do this for you.

Her Story
I remember growing up and hearing older people say, "let the visitors eat first," or "let the visitors go first."

I grew up in a "privileged" family since my Dad is a Pastor. Although my Dad never required it, people were mostly gracious to our family out of respect for my Dad. I remember when we visited the province, our family slept in the Master's bedroom while the homeowner slept somewhere else. It didn't matter if my Dad and Mom argued that we can sleep in one of the other rooms; the homeowner will not hear of it.

I also remember while on a mission's trip up in the mountains, our hosts offered their single, all-purpose room house for our group of young adults to sleep in while they slept in a relative's house nearby.

Pinoys would generally be hospitable to foreigners because they are visitors to the country.

14. Superstition

Various cultures have their own set of folklore, urban myths, and legends. Filipinos are no different. You might see some Pinoys jumping up and down when the New Year rings in. This is believed to make one grow taller.

During Christmas holidays, a basket of round-shaped fruits usually becomes the centerpiece on the dinner table. This is a tradition taken from the Chinese that is believed to bring luck and good fortune, especially money, for the coming year. Some also buy sticky sweets so the family stays sweet to each other and stick closer together.

If somebody drops a spoon or fork while eating, you might hear someone comment that the person who dropped the utensil will be expecting visitors soon.

As you get to know the Pinoy culture more, you'll hear more of these superstitious beliefs; some are funny and most of which are baseless. Superstitions vary depending on the island you visit.

Round fruits: The shape of the fruits symbolizes the shape of money (coin), which is believed to usher in wealth for the coming year.
Photo credit: Shella Joy Evale-Ruyeras

15. Pouty Point

Filipinos like to point by pouting their lips to a certain direction. No, they aren't trying to kiss you. If Malaysians point using their thumbs, Pinoys use their lips.

Usually, when your hands are full, you can point using your lips. And even if your hands weren't full and you just felt lazy, you would still use your lips.

His Story
This is a huge one for me! While in the Philippines, Chad and I were usually hand in hand down a busy street. We were trying to find a certain place. Chad asks this young man where such and such is. He smiles, says a few words, followed by pouty lips in our direction.

Now, where I come from people could get hurt for doing things like that! In my mind, he is either flirting with my girl by trying to kiss her or flirting with me! Not sure which one was worse at that time. I made sure he saw us holding hands by making it visible. That way, whomever he was going for, he would know they were taken! But as the conversation continued, I saw Chad had lips involved with her conversation as well. Their lip conversation finally ended. I was thankful yet confused as to what just happened, and so glad she was able to clear up my misconception.

40

Her Story

Pointing with the lips is sometimes an auto-response for some Pinoys. Especially, when someone asks you where something is, and it is right under your nose. It's a quirky Pinoy "thang."

16. Language Nuances

There are subtle differences in meaning when Pinoys say something in English that could mean different in Pinoy-speak. I'll give a few examples.

Bathroom, restroom, toilet, or the loo. Pinoys call it comfort room or CR for short. Although Pinoys understand bathroom, restroom, and toilet, you'll be pointed straight away to the right direction if you ask, "Where's the CR"?

Taking a "bath" in Pinoy-speak doesn't necessarily involve a bath tub. Although bath tubs are common in Philippine hotels, those are not what you would see in an average Pinoy home. Most bathrooms in Pinoy homes do not have tubs, and not all have shower heads. *Ligo* is the Pinoy word for bath. However, *ligo* encompasses everything from taking a shower; swimming in the river, pool, or ocean; getting wet in the rain; or taking a bucket of water outside the house to "bathe." So if someone tells you they are going to take a bath, erase the "soaking in a tub" image from your mind.

When asking the waiter/waitress for some napkin, it is better to ask for "tissue" or you might have your cheeks flushed from embarrassment when you are handed a feminine pad. Most might understand what you mean by napkin, but it is better to be safe than sorry.

Pinoys sometimes interchange the words he/she/him/her in a sentence. This is because only one non-gender word is used in Filipino, *sya*, which caters to males and females alike. When the speaker moves back and forth between he/she/him/her when referring to only one person, now you understand why.

Pronunciation
ligo */lee-goh'/*

Her Story
You might be surprised that table napkins (tissues) come in "Pinoy size." Pinoys don't use a lot of napkins when eating, even if they are eating with their hands. As with most things in the Philippines, the napkin size is smaller compared to the super-sized American. A small drink would be the equivalent of a child-sized drink in the US. A large drink is comparable to a medium-sized drink (US).

When using a public restroom in the Philippines, such as in a mall, do not expect toilet seat covers, tissues to wipe your bum, or napkins to wipe your hands with. You can probably buy some from a vending machine. Toilet use is free, thank God, but not the "extra" amenities.

This is a conversation I had with my husband the first few days we were married.
Edward: I thought you were taking a bath?

Me: Yep, I already did!
Edward: When?
Me: Just a few minutes ago.
Edward: And you're already done? How come the tub's not wet?
Me: Oh... I took a shower. <insert laughter here>
Edward: <confused> What? You said you were going to take a bath?

And that's when it hit me! And so I had some explaining to do. This was the first time I realized that in the US, taking a bath literally means soaking in the bath tub, of course! A shower is a shower, not a bath!

And you could imagine his reaction when I first told him I was going to take a half-bath. In his mind he thought... well, bathing the lower half of the body is probably doable, but how do you do the upper half without getting the lower half wet?

A Pinoy half-bath is taking a shower from the neck down, excluding the head. Why? Well, shampooing the hair takes longer, and you don't really want to go to bed with your hair wet. Half-baths are usually done in the evenings, while full baths (shower) are taken in the mornings.

17. Balikbayan Box

Aside from *pasalubong*, there is also the *balikbayan* box. Most likely, you'll know what a *balikbayan* box is after you marry your girlfriend, if it does go that route. This is a box of goodies that is sent by relatives living abroad to their family living in the Philippines. A medium-sized *balikbayan* box typically measures 18x18x24in.

A *balikbayan* box contains mostly common items that you probably won't think much of "gifting" people with, such as soap, lotion, coffee, canned goods, used clothing, bags, shoes, even make-up. The key word here is "imported." Anything that's not made in the Philippines--and especially if it's made in the US or a European country--are considered "luxury" items.

Her Story
Some Pinoys have made money selling used items sent by their relatives abroad. Some Pinoys pay a premium for items that come from outside the Philippines. The Pinoy mindset is that anything that's imported and made outside the Philippines is always better. Even if the same brand of soap, lotion, or gadget is made and sold in the Philippines, the non-Philippine made is thought of as "better quality," although not necessarily true.

Those who have relatives who send *balikbayan* boxes are considered the "lucky" ones for being able to own or wear stuff that's "from the US." It gives Pinoys bragging rights if the bag, shoes, shirt, watch, or whatever they are wearing is "from my relatives in the US" or "from my friend in London/Dubai/Singapore/Australia," and so on.

Balikbayan box: A box of goodies sent by relatives living abroad to their family living in the Philippines. The box can contain anything from food, clothes, purses, perfume, shoes, gadgets, and so on as long as it fits the box.

18. Smile! You're on Camera

Filipinos are a picture-happy breed. Point a camera in one direction and everyone crashes in to join, armed with smiles and a V (peace) sign. Pinoys do not shy away from striking a pose when a camera is pointed their way.

Wacky and Jump shots are a Filipino favorite. Wacky shots are when you make funny faces or poses. It doesn't matter how many tries it takes to capture the perfect jump shot as long as everybody is having a blast.

His Story

If you are not into pictures or taking pics, you will have to be patient and understanding with your Pinoy partner. Once the camera comes out, for them that's when the fun starts!

I am not much into pictures, but have to realize that what's important to her is important to me. If she cooks a meal, before we eat, a pic of the food has to be taken. If we go out to eat and our plates come to us steaming and smelling so good, she takes a pic of the food before we can eat. I have to be patient and endure 30 seconds of picture taking before I can eat... Now, that's love!

Jump Shot at Sundown

19. Eyebrows Up

Moving ones eyebrows up means "Yes" in non-verbal Filipino language. So, if you ask a question and you notice Filipinos twitching their eyebrows, they're saying "Yes" or "I agree with you."

His Story

In American culture, we normally answer Yes or No questions with the nodding or shaking of heads or using our vocal chords. I never in a million years thought one could use their eyebrows!

Communication skills have to be really developed and learned between the two different cultures. I'm not used to looking at eyebrows for a "Yes" or "I agree" answer. I usually take the upward motion of an eyebrow as a "What did you say?" or a "Could you repeat that?" You can imagine if I asked Chad a question and she keeps raising her eyebrows… finally saying, "didn't you see me say Yes?" The whole time I thought she wanted me to repeat the question!

It can be confusing, and at times comical.

20. Teasing

Teasing plays a good part in the Pinoy culture. You can be teased for a lot of things. The most common is teasing a guy to a girl to try to pair them off. This is very common for teenagers, but can really happen to anyone at any age. Foreigners visiting the Philippines who are single can expect to get teased. They can be teased to any single and available girl/guy. I've seen younger foreigners who got abhorred by being teased, and I've seen some who handled it well and just went with the flow.

Guys can also use teasing as a way to know if a girl likes them, based on her reactions when being teased. I know a guy who got the courage to ask a girl out based on her response when being teased to him. Depending on the person being teased, it can be a good thing. For example, someone can be teased by his friends that he is getting "fat" or a bit chubby, which may encourage him to lose off some of the weight.

Teasing helps you get grounded and stay modest and humble. Being conceited and bragging about stuff is probably one of the worst traits that Pinoys don't like. So if a Pinoy starts bragging about his accomplishments, he can be teased as "gay," "a coward," "ignorant," "a braggart," and so on just to keep him grounded.

Some foreigners may see this as Pinoys being nosy of

other people's business. There may be some truth to that, but teasing is usually done in a friendly banter and in a jolly or light mood, and never with strangers or people you hardly know.

21. Talk of the Town

I've heard comments from non-Filipinos that Pinoys love to gossip. I've heard it being said by a couple of foreigners that Gossip is a Filipino "past time." Now, I think that's taking it to the extreme. But as much as I hate to admit it, there may be some truth behind it.

Don't be surprised if you hear your girlfriend telling you juicy details about somebody else's "private" matter. And don't take it to heart either if somebody else knows what you thought was just between you and your girlfriend. Bottom line, if you don't want your girlfriend telling another person, let her know.

Her Story

I think gossiping is really the result of an idle mind. I don't think it is solely a Pinoy thing though. Other cultures have it too, except that most are probably better at keeping the gossip hush-hush. Everyone knows the rumor, but then everybody pretends they are unaware.

In the Pinoy setting, especially in a small town where everybody is on first name basis, everyone knows the rumor, and if asked, they will add in what they know. Pinoys won't pretend that they have no clue. Sometimes, it can be a "contest" of who knew first. The person who found out first gets the bragging rights.

22. Will you Marry Me?

Before you propose to your Filipina girlfriend, you should understand that it is Filipino culture for the guy to shoulder most, if not all of the wedding expenses. Especially if your girlfriend grew up in the province (country side), her parents would expect this.

In the Pinoy mindset, it is a way of showing your fiancee's family that she will be taken good care of after marriage. In the old days, the groom's family would give a dowry, such as a cow, to the bride's family to show their good intentions.

Although times have changed, and some working Pinays can shoulder the wedding expenses or both parties do 50-50, it is best to ask your girlfriend what her and her families' expectations are.

23. Small Talk / Pleasantries

When you visit your girlfriend in the Philippines for the second time and her relatives tell you that you've gotten "fat," don't be offended. Although calling people fat is rude, Filipinos simply take it with a grain of salt. It is a way of starting a conversation when you see someone you haven't seen for quite some time. If you did this same approach in the US, you may never see that person again.

If in Western countries you say "Hello, how are you?" A common Filipino greeting is "Hi, I noticed you gained/lost weight!" and that is putting it mildly in English terms.

Another common greeting is "Wow! You look like you haven't aged a bit!" or "Hi, you look even more beautiful/handsome now than the last time I saw you!"

Her Story

Some Pinoys can be brash with their comments, and it may seem like they are getting in your business. Mind you, these comments are not meant to belittle anyone. Pinoys are simply stating what they notice, and most of the time it is a genuine comment, compliment or not.

24. Hello, Eat

Another favorite Filipino greeting, especially when you are visiting someone at home is, "Hello, have you eaten yet?" (Tagalog: *Kumusta, kumain na kayo?* or Cebuano: *Kumusta, nika-on na mo?*) Filipinos are very hospitable and they always want their visitors to feel at home. When you are invited to a Filipino home you will most likely be served a meal if you visit during breakfast, lunch, or dinner time, and snacks if you visit any other time of the day. Serving food to visitors is a custom. It shows that the host is hospitable.

The average Filipino snack would be bread paired with coke or some other soft drink (soda). It is embarrassing to the host if you do not eat what is served to you. Even if you are not really that hungry, take a bite or two. Your hosts won't be offended if you don't finish everything off; there's always somebody else waiting for you to have your share first so they can have theirs.

Her Story

I remember ex-coworkers (pinoys) who were trained in the US complaining that they were invited over to an American co-worker's house, and they were offered nothing to eat, not even snacks. Pinoys expect food when they get invited over to a Filipino home, and in the same way offer food when they invite people over.

There may be times when friends drop by unannounced, which is typical. Almost always, you'll probably get a call or text a few hours/minutes before someone comes, or they just show up at your door unannounced. Because Filipinos are hospitable, it is a no-no to not let people in just because they did not inform you beforehand that they were coming. As customary, you have to offer something to eat. Doesn't have to be fancy as long as you have something.

25. Romantics at Heart

Love songs and ballads are the favorite music genre of Filipinos, including men. No, they're not gay, and it's not weird although it may seem odd to men from Western culture. This is very common especially during Karaoke/Videoke time, which is another favorite Filipino pastime.

His Story

I stayed on the top floor of a four-story apartment that had no hot water, which meant lots of cold bucket showers (shower head was not working). It also did not have AC, but at least I had an electric fan and my friend lizard that would crawl across the ceiling occasionally and scare me. The lizard and I had a mutual agreement. I would leave him alone if he would leave me be while I sleep. We got along great!

Every morning there was this rooster that persisted on waking me up. The rooster was not as nice to me as the lizard was! My window had a screen on it, but no glass (common in the Philippines). The rooster crowing was as clear as can be at the crack of dawn! You know you're in love when you're half way across the world, and cold water, lack of AC, lizards crawling, and roosters crowing don't seem to be bothersome.

The real test of love was on an early morning, after the

rooster finally shut up. I thought to myself, finally... peace and quiet. Then there was this loud, annoying noise coming from our neighbors. Construction workers have begun their day banging, hammering, drilling, and then they cranked up their music box! From those speakers came out love songs. Think Celine Dione and Mariah Carey.

Guys, for the most part, have a cool yet tough, manly exterior they like to portray. However, inside is hidden a secret softy, romantic teddy bear that only a girl, a little kid, or a baby can bring out.

The workers were sweatin', muscle-ripping, sledge-hammering away to Celine Dion's "My heart will go on." You got to be kidding me! I mean this kind of music needs to be played when you're out on a date or dancing with your girlfriend under the stars, but not with all your buddies using power tools!

I became really confused and deeply concerned for mankind. I asked my girlfriend, and you guessed it... with a smile and laughter she explained how it's part of culture. Once again, I accepted it, no problem. Our love will go on!

26. Bro-mance

Bro-mance is short for brotherly romance. It is used to call two straight guys who are best buds, and are always seen hanging out with each other, with or without their girlfriends.

Don't be alarmed if you see two Filipino guys walking down the street with one arm around the other's shoulders. Bro-mance is a regular sight and is not gay.

It is also common to see girls sitting close to each other, or walking and holding hands with their female friends.

Typically, Filipino gays are flamboyant, and look and dress like girls. Most are probably Transgender, as defined in Western cultures. But in the Philippines, transgenders and gays are the same and referred to as either *bayot* (cebuano), *bakla* (tagalog), or *bading* (slang). Both are obviously effeminate. You won't see the typical gay couple in Western countries where both dress, look, and act like men. In the same way, Pinoy lesbians look, dress, and act like men.

Pronunciation
bayot */bah-yoht/*; bakla */buck-la'/*; bading */bah-ding/*

Her Story
Sometimes, Pinoys tease their good friends as "gay" even if they are straight. Teasing is a part of the Filipino culture. (see #20)

27. Karaoke

As previously mentioned, Karaoke/Videoke is a favorite past time for Filipinos. Don't worry if you can't carry a tune, nobody will make fun of you. I know a lot of Filipinos who can't carry a tune, but still sing out loud during karaoke time, broken notes and all.

One sign that you are in a Filipino party is when karaoke is one of the party highlights.

Karaoke Time: Posing for the camera while our friend is singing.

28. Laugh Out Loud

When Filipinos get together, they can be loud and laugh a lot. They can reminisce about anything and everything under the sun, and laugh a lot! A get together with friends can last till the wee hours of the morning. Prepare yourself for a long and loud get together with family or friends.

Pinays, as well as some Pinoys have the knack for talking for hours and hours. This is typical if they haven't seen a friend for quite some time and now they are catching up on lost time.

Her Story
Talking non-stop takes talent. I'm not really the outgoing-saying-hello-to-everybody-or-talking-to-everyone-at-a-party type. But I can chit chat with my cousins and best friends 'till the wee hours of the morning. Phone or Skype conversations with my best friend living in the UK can last 2 to 3 hours at a time.

When one of my co-workers/friends came to visit me in the US, my husband said that we talked all day long, non-stop. He asked what we talked about and I replied, "Anything and everything."

29. Rich and Famous

Generally, foreigners, especially Caucasians are perceived to be "rich." Blame this to the influx of Hollywood movies and western TV shows.

You might enjoy a "celebrity" status just for being "white," especially if you visit the province (country side). Some may even wave at you or say hi, simply because you are "white."

Her Story
I have younger nieces who are part-Filipino, part-British. Whenever they visit the Philippines in the rural areas, they always feel like they are celebrities. Other kids (mostly neighbors) follow them around and simply stare at them just for looking different. I guess the Pinoy kids are simply curious. More often than not, the only "white" people they see are probably on TV or the movies. So it's like watching a live reality show.

In the urban setting though, you might not get followed around, but you may still get stares from curious onlookers.

30. Price of Fame

The perception that you are a foreigner and the "celebrity" status you enjoy comes at a price. When you invite your girlfriend and her family (which may include her extended family - grandma, grandpa, uncle, aunt, cousins, neighbors, etc.) out to eat, they expect you to pay the entire bill. You won't see anyone even "pretending" to pull out their wallets.

You might want to think twice before saying, "Let's go out to eat" if you are not ready to shoulder the entire bill. It is assumed, that you, the foreigner invited them, and therefore you should pay.

The same goes for friends. In the Filipino context, if you invite a friend out to eat, unless you state otherwise, you will pay for the meal. It is common with friends or even co-workers to ask if you will buy lunch/dinner/snacks, when you ask if they want to go grab a bite to eat. A common question asked is, *"bangka ka?"* (cebuano) or *"manglilibre ka?"* (tagalog), which when loosely translated simply asks if you will be buying the meal.

Pinoys, in general, don't take offense when asked, as buying somebody else's meals/snacks/drinks is common. Most Pinoys are generous, and I think the hospitable culture plays a part in this.

Pronunciation
bangka /*bung-kah*/; manglilibre /*mung-lee-lib-reh*/

31. Whitening Stuff

Filipinos who have lighter skin tone are generally perceived to be better-looking than *moreno/morena* or the *kayumanggi* (brown-skinned). This is the reason why a lot of Filipino actors and actresses are mestizos/mestizas, which is a term for bi-racial Pinoys.

Whitening lotions are common, and most Pinays want to have lighter skin. This is ingrained deeply in the culture way back when the Philippines was under Spain. The poor farmers, laborers, and so on toiled under the sun most of the day, which made their skin "dark" compared to their light skinned Spanish bosses who were indoors most of the time, and thus had "lighter" skin.

It is commonly perceived, albeit not a general truth, that those who work outdoors have a harder life than those who work in an office. White collar jobs are always seen as better and high-paying than blue collar ones.

This is also the reason why you might see some Pinays walking around with umbrellas on a bright sunny day. You will not see Pinays lying on the beach to get a tan. Pinoys go to the beach to swim, relax, have fun with friends and family, and eat, but not to get a tan!

Pronunciation
moreno /*moh-reh-noh*/; morena /*moh-reh-na*/; kayumanggi /*kah-you-mung-gi*/; mestizo /*mess-tea-soh*/; mestiza /*mess-tea-sah*/

Her Story
As a little girl, I thought that I was not as beautiful as my mestizo/mestiza cousins who inherited more of the Spanish gene from my Mom's side. I, on the other hand got my Dad's *moreno* skin tone.

Whenever we were out swimming at the beach, I was told by "well-meaning" relatives to stop being under the sun too much as I was getting dark, and that it would be difficult to see me at night. Thankfully, those comments didn't really do much to my self-esteem.

I was in my mid 20s when whitening lotions started to become a fad. We were bombarded with commercials on TV that promoted fairer skin as more beautiful than *kayumanggi*. Tag lines like *"Kutis mayaman, kahit saan mo pa tingnan"* (Loose translation: Skin like the rich, whichever way you look at) were splashed on billboards with bi-racial Pinoys promoting the whitening product.

Unfortunately, I bought into that deception. At one time, one of my besties and I even went to a spa for full body lightening! Obviously, nothing came out from that body lightening session, except me and my bestie having a great bonding time. We still have a good laugh when we talk about it.

When I started hanging out with non-Pinoys due to my work, that's when the whitening lotions stopped. It didn't matter anymore if I stayed under the sun and got more tan than I wanted, or if I got comments from friends of how "dark" I look. I've come to fully accept and love my brown skin.

While doing my research for this book, I have realized that this whitening phenomenon is not unique to the Philippines, but is common in Asia. Whitening products are huge in the Asian market.

Magazine ad for a whitening face lotion. (Model and product name intentionally blurred out.)

32. Birthday Treat

Whether you are celebrating your birthday or a promotion at work, it is expected that you treat your friends or coworkers to lunch/dinner. It is believed that since you have been blessed with another year, or blessed with a promotion that you should "share" your blessing with others.

A typical birthday greeting would be, "Happy birthday! Where's the party?" For promotions you'd hear, "Congratulations! Where are we going to eat?" Of course, it remains your choice if you want to buy or not, but if you don't, your friends may see you as being "stingy."

If one doesn't have a party at home, they will invite their close friends to eat out, and pay for the entire meal.

Typical Filipino food served during parties – Photo credit: Shella Joy Evale-Ruyeras

Boodle Fight – Photo credit: Shella Joy Evale-Ruyeras

33. Conservative

Filipinos are generally conservative in the way they think, talk, act, or dress. If you buy a bikini for your girlfriend to wear at the beach, it's highly likely (if she does wear it) that she will wear a shirt and shorts over it. Only a few Filipinas dare to bare at the beach where the typical swimming get up is a shirt and shorts.

At a typical beach resort, you won't see Pinays lying down on the sand, sunbathing in their bikini. As mentioned previously, Pinoys don't really care much for a tan. If not in the water, most are probably huddled up under a hut in their shorts and shirts, eating, chatting, and laughing the day away. That's what R&R (rest and relaxation) is in the Philippines.

If you do visit a tourist area, such as beach resorts in Boracay or Palawan, you will see some Pinay wearing bikini.

34. PDA

PDA or Public Display of Affection is not the norm. You won't see couples hugging, sitting on each other's lap, or openly kiss in public, and most especially not in front of their parents!

Even for married couples, holding hands in public is not common. This is due to the Filipino's conservative culture.

Her Story

Some pinoys, specially the elderly or conservatives, consider it being "vulgar" when they see a girl sitting on her boyfriend's lap. The girl is then labeled as being loose or someone with low moral values, and in worst cases, the girl can be labeled as a "prostitute" even when she is not.

35. Bless

One Filipino custom that you might be asked to do is *pagmamano*, which is taking an elderly person's hand and putting the back of the hand against your forehead. This is usually done by kids to their parents, grandkids to grandparents, nieces/nephews to their aunts/uncles, godkids to their godparents, or by a future son-in-law to his future parents-in-law. You get the gist.

Pagmamano shows a sign of respect, and it is sometimes called "bless," which is believed to obtain a "blessing" from the older person.

Pronunciation
pagmamano /*pug-mah-mah-noh*/

Her Story
I was not raised in a typical Filipino home where the kids would "bless" the parents. Instead, I gave my parents a kiss on the cheek when I left or arrived home from school. But whenever my family would visit relatives or attend a family reunion, I remember that I had to "bless" a lot of Uncles and Aunts, especially on my Dad's side. My Dad has 12 siblings, so you can just imagine that I had to bless, at least 12 uncles and aunts, their spouses, my grandparents, and other relatives who were much older than me. I got a lot of "blessings."

Pagmamano or "bless" shows a sign of respect, which is believed to obtain a "blessing" from the older person. — Photo credit: Meynard Simborio

36. Loud Voice

Don't be turned off if you hear your girlfriend talking to her siblings or her parents in a loud voice, as if they are arguing. Almost always, they are not. Loud is the "normal" talking voice, especially in the Visayas and Mindanao region. Filipinos are generally emotional and passionate folks, and they are very expressive when conversing in their dialect.

37. Confrontation

Filipinos avoid confrontation, if possible. If something rubs them the wrong way, they would rather suck it up, and complain in silence rather than make a big scene and lose face.

One example would be when you see Filipinos standing in line to withdraw from an ATM machine. Most Pinoys would not say anything if someone cuts in line, but you would definitely see from the facial expression or body language that they disliked it. However, if someone does gather enough courage and draws attention to it, it could readily turn into an ugly scene with everybody in line ganging up insults on the one who cut in line.

In a boyfriend-girlfriend relationship, this can become harmful. If your girlfriend simply gives you the cold shoulder and won't tell you what is wrong, this is because she is being non-confrontational. You have to encourage your girlfriend at all times to let you know if something bothers her no matter how trivial she thinks it is. You may have to prod her multiple times before you finally get an answer, but this will save your relationship from all the guess work (and drama).

38. Filipino Time

Almost all Filipinos observe Filipino time (except for school and work), which is 15 minutes to an hour late. If you made plans with your girlfriend and her friends to meet up at 9AM, don't be surprised if nobody shows up at 9, and most show up at 10, and no one is even apologizing for being late.

Everything follows Filipino time, even weddings (unless it is a wedding inside a Catholic church). If you're a stickler for time, prepare to be flexible with your schedule or it will drive you nuts!

Her Story

My friends and I agreed to meet at 9AM to go to the beach. It is typical for Filipinos to meet at one place, such as the mall or somebody's house, and then rent a van to go to the beach. As mentioned earlier, most Pinoys do not own vehicles. Typically, you would rent a van, or ride with a friend and go to the beach together.

One of our friends who was known for always showing up later than most texted that she was on her way. One friend quipped, "Is she on her way, riding a jeepney? on her way out the door? or on her way to take a bath?" We all had a good laugh.

Same goes if you watch a concert by a Pinoy celebrity. The

concert usually starts 30 mins to an hour after the scheduled time. Filipino time is commonly observed that Pinoys are accustomed to waiting.

39. Filipino Food

A typical Filipino diet consists of at most six meals a day: breakfast, snacks, lunch, snacks, dinner, and a midnight snack before bedtime. Rice is staple food and is usually eaten together with other dishes. For most Filipinos, a meal is not a meal without Rice. Pizza is a snack, not dinner.

Filipinos use spoon and fork when eating. The fork on the left hand is used to guide the food onto the spoon on your right, and then you bring the spoon to your mouth. Knives are rarely used when eating in a Filipino home. Some may eat with their hands, especially in informal settings, or when at the beach.

Popular dishes during celebrations are *adobo* (pork/chicken stew), *lumpia* (meat/vegetable rolls), *pancit* (noodles), *kinilaw* (ceviche or raw fish), *escabeche* (fish in sweet & sour sauce), and *lechon* (roasted pig). *Halo-halo* (crushed ice with milk, fruit, flan) is a favorite snack, and *leche* (milk) flan is a favorite dessert. The food preparation varies depending on the area you visit.

Pronunciation
adobo */uh-doh-boh/*; lumpia */loom-pyuh'/*; pancit */pun-sit/*; kinilaw */kee-knee-lahw/* escabeche */ehs-kah-beh-cheh/*; lechon */leh-chohn/*; halo-halo */huh-loh-huh-loh/*; leche */leh-cheh/*

Lechon or roasted pig is popular during birthdays, fiestas, weddings, and other life celebrations. The entire pig, with an apple in its mouth usually becomes the table centerpiece.

40. Gratitude to Parents

Children who are all grown up are expected to take care of their elderly parents. It shows gratitude to the parents for taking care of the children when they were growing up, and for sending them to school. Putting one's parents up in a nursing home is a big no-no. Only those who do not have family end up in homes for the elderly in the Philippines. It is considered to be disrespectful to even consider putting your elderly parents in a nursing home.

Taking care of elderly parents is usually done by the oldest child, but some families take turns, and elderly parents live a year with one child, and the next year with another. Older people are highly respected, even if they are strangers.

41. Bayanihan

This is a word taken from *Bayan*, which means country, town, or community in general. Typically, *Bayanihan* is a term used when a community gets together for a common cause.

In the old days when Filipino houses were on stilts made of nipa huts, and a family wanted to move to another town, the whole neighborhood would come together, lift the house up on their shoulders, and relocate the house.

Bayanihan is still practiced in communities getting together to beautify their community, or build a communal basketball court, and so on.

Pronunciation
bayan /*bah-yun*/; bayanihan /*bah-yah-knee-hun*/

42. Pamamanhikan
If you and your girlfriend are planning to get married, it is the culture to ask the parents for your girlfriend's hand. This is referred to as *pamamanhikan* in Tagalog or *pamalaye* in Cebuano.

This is usually done at the girl's house, and is simply a formality where you ask the girl's parents for her hand, and state your intentions for marrying her. The parents then agree to your wedding plans and give their blessing. This is also a chance for the parents, especially the Dad (unless he is non-confrontational) to ask questions to make sure that his daughter would be taken good care of.

As with other Pinoy activities, there will be food served afterwards to celebrate the "agreement." You and your girlfriend are now "officially" engaged.

Pronunciation
pamamanhikan */Pah-mah-mun-he-cun/*; pamalaye */pah-mah-lah-ye/*

Hot seat: My husband's pamalaye/pamamanhikan w/ my parents.

The Girl

43. Soap Opera
Some Filipinas like drama in a relationship, and would even go to the extent of "creating" the drama, such as exaggerate or blow things out of proportion. Pinays are (generally) "jealous" girlfriends. They will create drama if they "feel" that their foreigner boyfriend is being friendly towards another Filipina. I've had non-Filipino friends gripe about this.

As long as you do not give your girlfriend a chance to doubt your loyalty to her, you will not have this problem.

Her Story
Now that my husband and I are married, I've heard from non-Filipinos married to Pinays that although their wives are very loving, caring, thoughtful, and always seeing to their every need, they can be a bit possessive. It's difficult for the husband to grasp why his Pinay wife becomes "jealous" with him having a simple conversation with another girl.

I asked my girlfriends' (married to foreigners or pinoys) opinion on this matter and almost everyone pointed out that jealousy or rather not being jealous comes with maturity. Obviously, if your pinay girlfriend is young (think early 20s), her tendency to get jealous is higher than if she were older because at that young age she is not yet sure of herself, or has yet to build self-confidence/self-assurance. Also, this does not apply to Pinays only, but to younger men/women in general.

One thing that could add to the fire of jealousy is the Pinoy culture of gossip. What could have been a simple conversation is now turned into a flirtatious conversation as it goes down the rumor mill. Failing to understand your partner's culture is a good part of failing to understand who they are. The Pinay's culture is very much a part of who she is.

Although it should go both ways, but as the man pursuing a relationship, I believe the guy should take the more understanding role.

Bottom line, you won't have to worry about a jealous girlfriend if you don't give your girlfriend a reason to get jealous, and have open communication.

44. He said, She Said

Expect communication problems due to the language difference, regardless if you think your girlfriend speaks better English than the average Filipina (she may work in a call center, etc.).

Conversational English is different from written English, and the English taught in Philippine schools is the more formal, written English. Some words are also pronounced differently or the stress is on a different syllable.

Also, if your girlfriend grew up speaking the native tongue, she most likely also thinks in the native tongue. Thinking in the native tongue, translating your thoughts, and then expressing them in English can be quite a challenge.

In addition, there are a lot of Filipino words that are specific to the language and do not have an equivalent English word. To ease the communication gap, learn to speak slowly and listen intently. Don't jump into conclusions right away. Ask your girlfriend what she really means with what she said.

45. Single Living with Parents

What? You're 28 and you still live with your parents?

Don't be surprised if your girlfriend still lives with her single siblings and parents under one roof. It is common for single Pinoys to live with their parents. Unless, your girlfriend is from the province (country side), and moved to study or work in the big city, she most likely still lives with her parents.

Some Filipino families are closely-knit that an extended family of uncles, aunts, cousins, grandmas, and grandpas all live under one roof or their houses are right next to each other.

46. Yaya

A *yaya* is a personal helper who typically helps around the house. Hiring household help is common in middle-class families, and rich families may have two or more *yayas*, or one for each kid.

My husband found it interesting that somebody else had to do all the cooking, cleaning, washing, and ironing for me. He calls me his "princess" because I did not know anything about doing household chores since I grew up with a *yaya*.

Yayas are considered to be part of the family. In most rich families, the *yaya* and her entire family are hired to help out. Some even bring their *yayas* to vacation with them when they travel outside the country.

Pronunciation
yaya */yuh-yuh/*

Her Story
My husband and I finally met in person when he flew to visit me in the Philippines. I was 34, living by myself, with a *yaya*. He met my parents (who flew in from California), as well as my *yaya's* husband who was my car mechanic, and their daughter who we helped send to school. In my defense, I do know how to cook, clean, and so on since my Mom made sure I learned them even if I had a *yaya*, but

my "domestic" skills were not up to par until I married my husband. Don't let *yayas* scare you though. Most Filipinos don't have *yayas*.

Some Things to Consider

47. Real Filipina
If you're in the Philippines looking to date a "real" Filipina, and by that I mean somebody who was born female, then beware of "girls" with wide wrists and big hands. Generally, Filipino men have smaller frames than their foreign counterparts, and can easily be mistaken as females if they dress and look the part. The hands are a clear giveaway. Pinays have much smaller and delicate hands. Also, the average Pinay height is 5' (and below). Be wary if the "Pinay" is 5'6" which is the average Pinoy height. To be safe, look for the Adam's apple (some gays can be very good at hiding them though).

Gays are common in the Philippines. Some towns even have gay pageants. Most Pinoys have a "gaydar," (gay radar) and can easily detect a gay pinoy. If you are unsure, you can always ask another Pinoy (even a stranger), and they won't hesitate to tell you the truth. I think most gays themselves will tell you that they are gay (if you ask nicely), just so that there is no misunderstanding.

Her Story
An expat coworker/friend told me that during his first week in the Philippines, he was hitting the bars, and was flirting heavily with some lady. He then told the Pinoy coworkers he was hanging out with that he was ready to

call it a night and take the lady home. Our coworker said that was fine, and then casually mentioned, "you do know she's a he, right?"

You could just imagine his reaction, red face and all! I taught him the hands, wrists, and Adam's apple trick, and his gaydar improved drastically.

48. Street Food

If you have a delicate tummy, it's best to stay away from food that you are not accustomed to. Home cooked meals or food ordered from restaurants are mostly safe to eat. Be wary of street food, which is any food sold in the streets, whether from a food cart or somebody's food basket. I'm not saying all street food is bad, as I'm an avid fan of fish ball dipped in special sweet sauce, and dirty ice cream (it's not really dirty, that's the name for ice cream sold in the streets).

However, if you're more the adventurous type who likes to try different cuisines, then go ahead and dive in. Just make sure you politely ask what it is you are about to eat. You could be eating pig's blood (*dinuguan*), a favorite Filipino staple during fiestas or chicken feet, chicken head, pig intestines, pig tongue (*lengua*), *balut* (boiled duck egg w/ embryo), and so on.

Don't worry because these are not the typical Filipino food served to foreign visitors. These are more the exotic food that you can buy in the streets. I'm Filipino yet I don't eat most of the above, except for *balut*.

Simple rule: Ask before you eat.

Pronunciation
dinuguan /*dee-noo-goo-un*/; lengua /*lehng-gwuh*/; balut

/buh-loot/ or */buh-loht/*

Fishbal l/Tempura cart

49. Bottled Water

Drink bottled water at all times, no exception. Even locals do it. Filipinos mostly refer to bottled water as "mineral water."

Her Story

I am not sure how often tap water tests are conducted in the Philippines, and if water quality meets international standards.

Although some Pinoys may be immune to the water contaminants (if any), non-Pinoys may not be as lucky.

50. Plug-In Ready

Bring a universal outlet if you plan on taking your phone or other techie gadgets, such as a laptop. Outlets in the Philippines are dual slots only. You may also need to bring a converter if you plan on bringing your electric shaver or other gadgets. If you're over your luggage limit and can't pack them, these items can be easily bought at an electronics store inside the mall, that is if you are visiting a city and not a rural (country side) area.

Electric voltage in the Philippines is 220v, and would easily fry a gadget that runs on 110v. Always check your gadget's voltage before plugging it in.

His Story

I took a converter with me ahead of time because Chad warned me about the power difference. Although I had it with me, one evening I was shaving, wondering why my electric shaver was about to blow up in my hand. When it started smoking I realized I forgot to plug it into the converter. Converters aren't expensive and very much needed.

Frying your gadgets would be bad; burning your GF's building down would be worse!

About the Authors
Edward and Chad Moss
Larry Edward Moss aka Edward serves as the youth pastor of Living Word Church in McDonough, GA. His wife, Charlyn Lez Dumanon-Moss aka Chad works as a Technical Writer. Although they were raised continents apart, both share a common upbringing in that they are both Pastor's kids. Their love story, though not the norm, has inspired people and blasted the notion that online dating is only for geeks, the weird, and the desperate. Both believe that with any relationship, there has to be open communication and honesty, with Christ as the foundation so it will stand strong and endure the tests of time.

If you have any specific questions about the Philippines, please reach out to us at chad.pink@yahoo.com and we'll try our best to answer them.

Love Story in a Nutshell
At 34 years of age, Chad signed up on a dating site to appease her worried, but well-meaning Mom who had been prodding her for two years! She received an unsolicited email from a Christian dating site with a tag line that caught her attention: Let His heart lead yours!

Edward, 30 at that time, heard the same tag line over the radio. And although not much of a "computer person" decided to give it a try after being fed up with a few failed relationships.

Within a week or so of signing up, Edward saw Chad's picture scroll by and clicked it. He sent her a wink, and she sent a wink back, which started a year of e-mailing, phone calls, and skyping, to eventually meeting each other after a year.

During those couple of weeks in the Philippines, Edward asked for Chad's hand from her parents (pamalaye), and then did a not-so-smooth proposal on top of a 40 storey building with a bus-load of noisy, camera-clicking Japanese tourists.

After a few months of processing her visa, Chad came to the US and the couple got married in California where Chad's parents and most of her relatives reside.

Edward and Chad currently reside in Georgia with their four year old son.

Printed in Great Britain
by Amazon